First published in Canada and the United States in 2022
Text copyright © 2022 Laura Alary
Illustration copyright © 2022 Andrea Blinick
This edition copyright © 2022 Pajama Press Inc.
This is a first edition.
10 9 8 7 6 5 4 3 2 1

www.pajamapress.ca   info@pajamapress.ca

Canada Council   Conseil des arts
for the Arts   du Canada

ONTARIO ARTS COUNCIL
CONSEIL DES ARTS DE L'ONTARIO
an Ontario government agency
un organisme du gouvernement de l'Ontario

Canada

The publisher gratefully acknowledges the support of the Canada Council for the Arts and the Ontario Arts Council for its publishing program. We acknowledge the financial support of the Government of Canada through the Canada Book Fund (CBF) for our publishing activities.

Library and Archives Canada Cataloguing in Publication
Title: Sun in my tummy / by Laura Alary ; illustrated by Andrea Blinick.
Names: Alary, Laura, author. | Blinick, Andrea, 1979- illustrator.
Description: First edition.
Identifiers: Canadiana 20210303212 | ISBN 9781772782417 (hardcover)
Classification: LCC PS8601.L264 S86 2022 | DDC jC813/.6—dc23

Publisher Cataloging-in-Publication Data (U.S.)
Names: Alary, Laura, author. | Blinick, Andrea, 1979-, illustrator.
Title: Sun in My Tummy / by Laura Alary ; illustrated by Andrea Blinick.
Description: Toronto, Ontario Canada : Pajama Press, 2021. | Summary: "In simple but expressive free verse, a mother describes to her young daughter how the sun's light becomes the energy in her body through the oats, blueberries, and milk in her home-cooked breakfast. An Author's Note with more age-appropriate detail about photosynthesis is included"— Provided by publisher.
Identifiers: ISBN 978-1-77278-241-7 (hardback)
Subjects: LCSH: Plants – Effect of light on -- Juvenile literature. | Nutrition -- Juvenile literature. | Children – Health and hygiene. | Photobiology – Juvenile literature. | BISAC: JUVENILE NONFICTION / Science & Nature / Flowers & Plants. | JUVENILE NONFICTION / Health & Daily Living / Diet & Nutrition. | JUVENILE NONFICTION / Science & Nature / Chemistry.
Classification: LCC QP141.A453 |DDC 612.3 – dc23

Original art created with gouache, colored pencil, collage, and chalk pastel
Cover and book design— Lorena González Guillén

Manufactured in China by WKT Company

Pajama Press Inc.
11 Davies Avenue, Suite 103 Toronto, Ontario Canada, M4M 2A9

Distributed in Canada by UTP Distribution
5201 Dufferin Street Toronto, Ontario Canada, M3H 5T8

Distributed in the U.S. by Ingram Publisher Services
1 Ingram Blvd. La Vergne, TN 37086, USA

For my dad, who put the sun
in my tummy every morning

—L.A.

For my two sunshines,
Mara and Ruby

—A.B.

You wake up in the dark.
The blankets hug you tight
and you snuggle deeper.
It can't be time to get up yet.
But it is.
Time to put the sun in your tummy.

In the kitchen, a pot of water
bubbles on the stove.
In goes the oatmeal.
Here comes the sun!

Not long ago,
these oats were a field
of swaying grasses.

Before that, seeds,
snuggled deep in the dark earth,
like you in your blankets.
What woke them?
The sun!
It tickled those sleepy little seeds
and called them to rise and shine.

They were hungry and thirsty
so they gobbled food from the soil
and drank rain from the clouds.

Bursting out of their cozy seed coats,
they stretched up and up, reaching for the sun,
while their roots went down into the earth.

Those oats grew tall and green,
then turned to gold.
Hidden inside were all the things
that had made them grow.

Clouds. Rain. Soil. Sun.
They're hard to see. But look deeper.
Everything is there.

What's next?

Blueberries!

Once they grew wild
on low bushes with
smooth green leaves.
Inside those leaves,
real magic happened.

It began with the sun,
who showers the earth
with heat and light—
tiny packets of energy.

You can feel its warmth on your skin.
But green plants can do something more.
Something amazing.

The leaves of that blueberry bush
caught the sun energy and used it
to break apart gases in the air.

Then they put the pieces back together
to make something new: sugar.

Food from thin air!

When the time was right
those blueberry bushes
burst into bloom.
Bees, birds, and butterflies
flitted from flower to flower.
Deep inside each blossom,
seeds began to form.
Around the seeds,
soft and juicy coats.

These are the berries.
Sugar-sweet.
Some of them were gobbled up
by birds and animals.
Others dropped to the ground.
When seeds go to back to the soil
they make new plants,
which make more seeds,
which make more plants.
On and on it goes.
Do you see?

The bush. The blossoms. The green leaves.

The sun and air they use to make their sweet magic.

All the plants and seeds that came before.

All the plants and seeds that might grow someday.

Everything is there in each blueberry.

Try one. Is it sweet?

Is that the taste of sunlight?

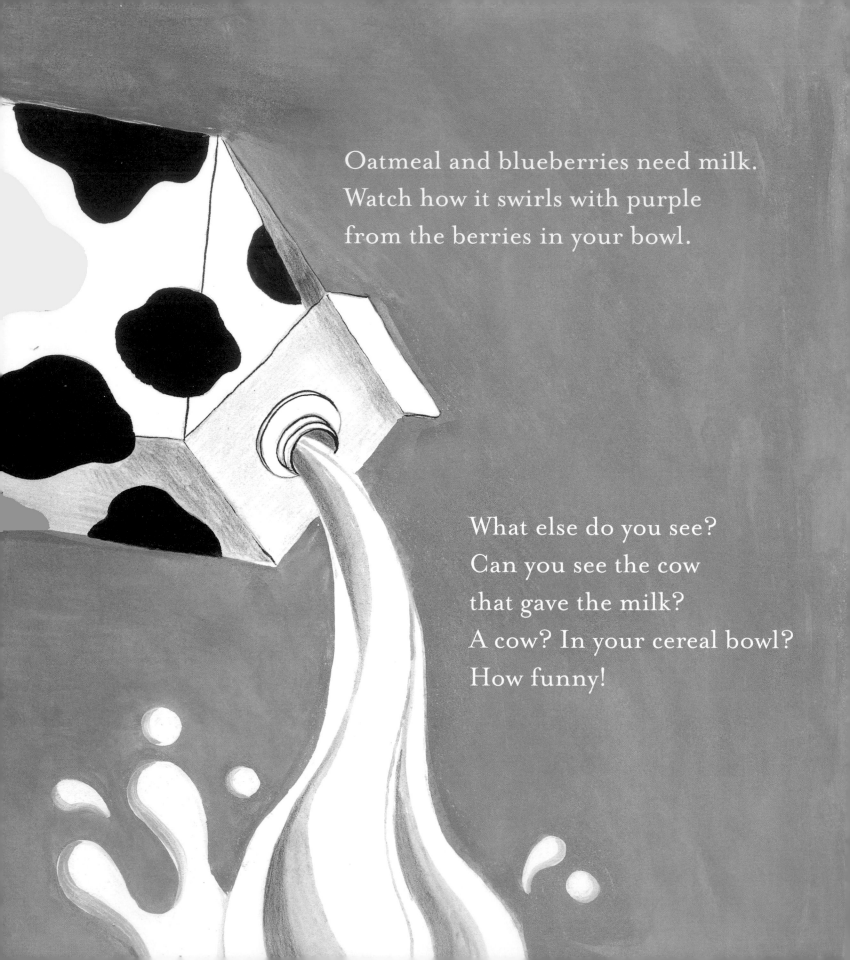

Oatmeal and blueberries need milk.
Watch how it swirls with purple
from the berries in your bowl.

What else do you see?
Can you see the cow
that gave the milk?
A cow? In your cereal bowl?
How funny!

Picture her munching
sweet green grass,
that grew in soil,
watered by rain,
that came from clouds,
formed by oceans,
warmed by the sun.

And inside every blade of grass,
that same magic—
food made from air and sunlight,
for you and every living thing.
All of it is there in every drop of milk.

Inside everything,
if you look
deep enough,
you will find
the sun.

Warm-hearted.
Generous.
Giving.

Take a big spoonful.
Does it warm you from the inside?
Can you feel the glow spreading
through your body?
You are awake now, ready for a new day.
You have the sun in your tummy.

AUTHOR'S NOTE

If you had come to earth billions of years ago, you would not have felt at home. There was no oxygen in the atmosphere, so you would not have been able to breathe. The only life on earth were tiny bacteria living in the seas.

But something amazing happened.

Some of those little bacteria found a way to make their own food. They used energy from sunlight to break apart the water in the seas (which was made of hydrogen and oxygen) and carbon dioxide in the atmosphere (which was made of carbon and oxygen), and put the bits back together to make something new—sugar! This process is called *photosynthesis*.

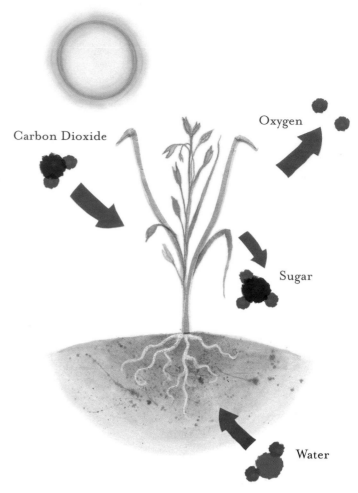

Those clever little bacteria became the ancestors of green plants. They moved onto the land, digesting rock, creating soil, and preparing the way for other life forms. They even created our atmosphere. When photosynthesis happens there is a lot of oxygen left over. This was a huge problem at first because oxygen was poisonous to the bacteria. But eventually some of them figured out how to use it. Many of their descendants became bigger and more complicated life forms—ones that needed oxygen to live and grow. This includes you!

In time the earth was covered with green and growing things. There were insects to pollinate them and birds and other animals to eat their fruit and spread their seeds. All of them were connected, and they all depended on energy from the sun.

Sun in My Tummy uses the word *magic* to describe how plants turn air and water and sunlight into food. This is not really magic. It is chemistry—part of how our world works. But that doesn't make it any less amazing. So any time you take a breath, or have a snack, or sit down for a meal, thank green plants and the sun for making it all possible.

—LAURA ALARY

For more resources, visit pajamapress.ca/book/sun_in_my_tummy